W9-CNQ-439

HOW DID WE FIND OUT ABOUT
ANTARCTICA?

HOW DID WE FIND OUT . . . SERIES
Each of the books in this series on the history of
science emphasizes the process of discovery.

How Did We Find Out . . . ?
Books by Isaac Asimov

HOW DID WE FIND OUT ABOUT

ANTARCTICA?

Isaac Asimov
Illustrated by David Wool

WALKER AND COMPANY
New York

To Nanette and Julio and to their happiness

Library of Congress Cataloging in Publication Data

Asimov, Isaac, 1920-
How did we find out about Antarctica?

(How did we find out . . . series)
Includes index.
SUMMARY: Describes the geography of the Antarctic
regions and the history of their discovery and exploration.
1. Antarctic regions—Juvenile literature.
[1. Antarctic regions] I. Wool, David. II. Title.
G863.A74   1979   998   79-2199
ISBN 0-8027-6370-7
ISBN 0-8027-6371-5 lib. bdg.

First published in the United States of America
in 1979 by the Walker Publishing Company, Inc.

Published simultaneously in Canada by Beaverbooks,
Limited, Pickering, Ontario.

TRADE ISBN: 0-8027-6370-7
REINF. ISBN: 0-8027-6371-5

Library of Congress Catalog Card Number: 79-2199

Printed in the United States of America

10 9 8 7 6 5 4 3 2 1

Contents

ADÉLIE PENGUINS

1 South Around the Continents

THE ANCIENT GREEKS, by about 300 B.C., were quite sure that the earth was a globe, a round ball. They knew it had a North Pole at one end, a South Pole at the other, and the line of the equator exactly in between.

None of the Greeks had ever been to the North Pole or to the South Pole, or even to the equator. The Greek scholars knew those places had to be there just the same.

They could tell from the fact that the sun was always in the southern part of the sky that all the lands they knew lay north of the equator.

Could there be land south of the equator, too?

Some Greek scholars thought there must be. They felt that it was only reasonable to suppose that if there was land north of the equator, there ought to be land south of the equator, too.

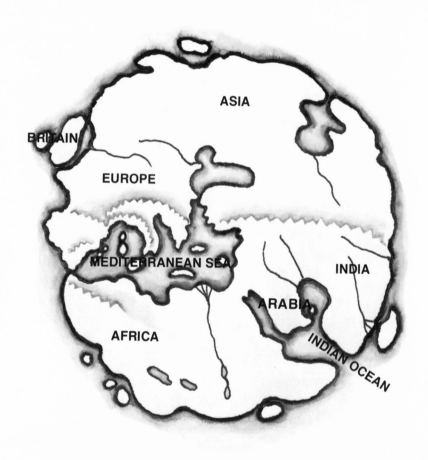

GRAECO-ROMAN VIEW OF THE WORLD

But, then, it might be impossible ever to visit the land south of the equator. The farther south one traveled, the hotter it was. Many people thought that near the equator it would be too hot for human beings to survive.

In that case the two sides of the earth would be forever separate. The northerners could not visit the southerners; nor could the southerners visit the northerners.

Of course, we now know there *are* lands south of the equator. We know that there have been people living on those lands since very ancient times. In fact, human beings may even have first come into existence on land south of the equator.*

The Greeks didn't know about that, however, and they never found out. They could only think about it. The Romans didn't find out, either. Nor did the Europeans in the Middle Ages.

Even as late as 1420 no European had ever been as far south as the equator.

By the 1400s Europeans were very anxious to find a way to get to India and to the lands and islands to the east of India. From those eastern lands came such things as cotton, silk, sugar, spices, and many other things Europeans wanted to have. Those things had to come long distances through various nations. Each nation charged a tax, and by the time the products

---

*See How Did We Find Out About Our Human Roots (New York: Walker, 1979).

reached western Europe, they were very expensive.

The most western European nation was Portugal, and the eastern products were most expensive there. In 1418 a Portuguese prince named Henry got an idea. Why not go to India by sea? Why not sail around Africa and get to India?

HENRY THE NAVIGATOR

Of course no one knew how large Africa was or how far south it stretched, but there was only one way to find out. Send ships.

Henry established a center for navigation at the southwestern tip of Portugal. From it he began sending out ships. Each one went a little farther down the coast of Africa than the one before had gone.

Henry, who came to be called Henry the Navigator, died in 1460. By that time the Portuguese ships had sailed a couple of thousand miles along the African coast, but they were still far from the equator. They hoped they would find that Africa didn't stretch as far as the equator and that they could get around Africa without getting into the area of terrible heat.

For a while, the African coastline turned east well north of the equator, but then it turned south again. In 1482 a Portuguese navigator, Diogo Cão (KOWN) finally reached the equator and passed beyond. He was the first European to do so.

He found out two things. First, the equator wasn't unbearably hot. It could be reached and passed. Second, there was land south of the equator, for Africa stretched beyond it.

In 1488 another Portuguese navigator, Bartholomeu Dias (DEE-us), reached the Cape of Good Hope, the southern tip of Africa. In 1497 still another Portuguese navigator, Vasco da Gama (GAM-a), went all around Africa and reached India.

How far south did Africa extend?

The distance north and south is measured in equal "degrees of latitude" (LAT-ih-tood). The equator is at 0 degrees, usually written 0°. The distance between the equator and the North Pole is divided into ninety parts so that the North Pole is 90 degrees north latitude, or 90° N. Halfway from the equator to the North Pole would be 45° N; two thirds of the way would be 60° N, and so on.

In the same way, the South Pole is 90 degrees south latitude, or 90° S. Halfway from the equator to the South Pole is 45° S; two thirds of the way is 60° S, and so on.

The southern tip of Africa is at about 35° S. That is only a little over a third of the way from the equator to the South Pole.

While the Portuguese navigators were trying to get around Africa, Christopher Columbus, an Italian navigator, had another idea. Since the world was round, he might be able to reach India by sailing west from Europe. The route to India might be shorter that way than by sailing around Africa.

Spain supplied Columbus with three ships, and he sailed westward in 1492. He discovered the American continent and thought it was India, but it wasn't. After a while people realized that the world was larger than Columbus had thought. He had discovered brand new continents, and India lay far beyond.

Spain was dissatisfied. Portugal was doing all

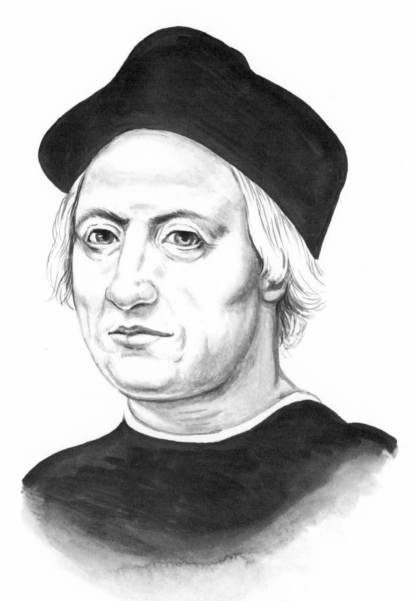

CHRISTOPHER COLUMBUS

the trading with India and other places in Asia, and Spain wasn't.

A Portuguese navigator, Ferdinand Magellan (muh-JELL-an), had been ill treated by the Portuguese government, and he decided to sail for Spain instead. It was his idea to get past the American continents somehow and to continue to sail westward to India.

In 1519 Magellan left Spain to look for a way past the American continents. It wasn't easy, for the American continents seemed to be solid land from all the way north to all the way south.

Finally, when Magellan had gone quite far south, he came to an inlet of water on October 21, 1520. He entered it and continued along through very bad weather and storms. It *did* lead him to the other side of the American continent, and to this day it is called the Strait of Magellan in his honor.

At the other end of the strait, Magellan came out into another ocean where the sun was shining and there were no storms. He called it the "Pacific", or "peaceful", Ocean.

The Strait of Magellan is at about 54° S. It is three fifths of the way from the equator to the South Pole.

What's more, south of the Strait of Magellan is another piece of land. When they were going through the strait, the sailors on Magellan's ships could see campfires there, so they called the land "Tierra del Fuego" (tee-ER-uh-del-fyoo-AY-goh), or "land of fire."

Magellan paid no attention to Tierra del Fuego. He just wanted to get through the strait and go on to India. He didn't make it himself. He died in the Philippine Islands, but the survivors kept on going.

On September 8, 1522, just one of Magellan's original five ships arrived home safely. There were only eighteen men left on board. They had been the first people ever to circumnavigate (sail all around) the earth.

Some geographers remembered the ancient Greek speculations about land south of the equator. They didn't think that it could be just the southern parts of Africa or South America. That wasn't enough. They thought there should be as much land south of the equator as there was north of it. They felt there should be continents there as big as Asia or even bigger.

Perhaps Tierra del Fuego was part of that continent. They drew maps of the globe with an imaginary big continent of which Tierra del Fuego was part.

Toward the end of 1577 the English navigator Francis Drake set off for the Pacific coast of South America.

England and Spain were practically at war in those days, and daring English navigators could get rich by looting the Spanish possessions in the Americas. Spain stood guard over the Atlantic coastline of the Americas, but they thought the Pacific coastline was safe. And so it was left unguarded.

FERDINAND MAGELLAN

MAGELLAN'S SHIP VICTORIA

Drake passed through the Strait of Magellan, and by September 6, 1578, he was in the Pacific Ocean. Then a storm struck him and drove him south. He was pushed sufficiently far south to let him see that Tierra del Fuego was an island. South of it was open sea.

That stretch of sea is now known as Drake Strait.

SIR FRANCIS DRAKE

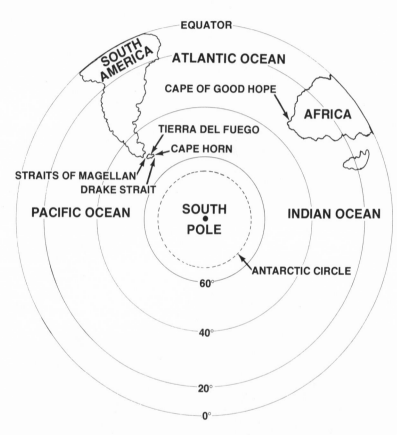

LAND SOUTH OF THE EQUATOR
KNOWN IN 1578

EQUATOR

SOUTH AMERICA

ATLANTIC OCEAN

CAPE OF GOOD HOPE

AFRICA

TIERRA DEL FUEGO

CAPE HORN

STRAITS OF MAGELLAN

DRAKE STRAIT

PACIFIC OCEAN

SOUTH
• POLE

INDIAN OCEAN

ANTARCTIC CIRCLE

60°

40°

20°

0°

There were people who lived on the island of Tierra del Fuego. What no one knew at this time was that this was the most southerly piece of land on which people lived and which they called home. The southern tip of Tierra del Fuego is Cape Horn, and that is at about 56° S.

Drake didn't pause to do any exploring. He

18

was after loot. He picked up all his ship could carry along the Pacific coast of the Americas. Then he crossed the Pacific and went home to England. He was the second man to circumnavigate the earth.

2 South to the Antarctic Circle

EVEN AFTER people knew that Tierra del Fuego wasn't part of a continent, they still believed a southern continent existed somewhere.

The logical place for it to be was somewhere in the Pacific Ocean. By the 1600s the geographers knew the real size of the globe, thanks to Magellan and Drake. They knew where the American shorelines were on the west and where the Asian and African shorelines were on the east.

Between the Americas on one side and Asia and Africa on the other was an ocean that stretched more than halfway around the world. People couldn't believe that all that vast area was just water. They felt there must be huge unknown continents located somewhere in it. Navigators began to look for those continents.

Southeast of Asia were large islands called the East Indies. Were any of them really part of a continent?

In 1602 a Spanish navigator, Luis Vaez de Torres (TAWR-rays) sailed round those islands and checked their coastlines. They were all islands. None was big enough to be a continent. The largest of the East Indies was the easternmost island, which was called New Guinea (nyoo-GIN-ee).

Torres explored the southern coast of that island, and the waters off that southern coast are called Torres Strait in his honor. He did not see any of the large body of land that lay immediately south of Torres Strait.

In the year of Torres's voyage Dutch navigators and merchants had taken over the East Indies. Although Torres had not seen any land, vague reports about such land began to reach the Dutch.

In 1642 the governor general of the East Indies, Anton van Diemen (van-DEE-men) sent an exploring expedition southward under Abel Janszoon Tasman (TAZ-man).

Tasman had amazingly bad luck. In the course of a ten-month voyage he managed to sail all around a piece of land as large as the whole United States without ever seeing it.

However, he managed to find smaller islands near that very large one. To the southeast of the land he missed, Tasman discovered an island he named Van Diemen's Land after the governor

ABEL JANSZOON TASMAN

23

general. Many years later, however, it was re-named Tasmania (taz-MAY-nee-uh) after the discoverer.

Farther to the southeast Tasman discovered two larger islands, which he called New Zealand after the Dutch province of Zeeland.

On a later voyage, in 1644, Tasman did detect the northern shores of the large land he had missed before. There were also vague additional reports. The Dutch called this new land New Holland but didn't know much about it.

None of these sightings satisfied those who were hoping for a large southern continent.

Some people were sure that there must be a southern continent surrounding the South Pole and bulging up far into the Pacific. It might be difficult to sail the vast Pacific and hope to bump into the continent just by chance. Why not sail south instead? A ship would be sure to find the continent that way, and then it could just follow its shores up through the Pacific Ocean.

In 1738 a French navigator, Pierre Bouvet de Lozier (boo-VAY-duh-loh-ZYAY), headed southward from the southern tip of Africa. It was the first voyage that was meant to do nothing more than look for the southern continent. All he uncovered was a small island that is still called Bouvet Island in his honor.

Another French navigator, Yves Joseph de Kerguelen-Tremarec (ker-gay-LEN-tray-ma-REK), set out in 1771. He probed south of Africa too and found nothing but another island, now known as Kerguelen Island (KER-guhlen).

Neither Bouvet Island nor Kerguelen Island was as far south as Cape Horn. That remained the most southerly piece of land known.

At sea, however, was the greatest navigator of them all, an Englishman, James Cook, known to everybody as Captain Cook.

Between 1768 and 1771, on the first of three great voyages, Captain Cook sailed across the South Pacific Ocean and explored the coasts of New Guinea, New Holland, and New Zealand.

He was able to show exactly what Tasman had missed. New Holland was the largest island in the world. It is so large that it is usually considered a continent. Captain Cook called it Australia (aws-TRAY-lee-uh) from the Latin word for south. The name makes sense. Africa and South America are each larger than Australia, but each is only partly south of the equator. Australia is entirely south of the equator. It was the largest piece of land that anyone had yet found that was wholly south of the equator.

But was there nothing more? Might there not be an even larger continent in the vastness of the Pacific?

In 1772 Captain Cook set off on a second expedition to see if anything at all existed in the widest part of the Pacific Ocean, the part south of the equator. He searched the ocean thoroughly and showed beyond any doubt that there was no piece of land that was continental in size in the South Pacific except for Australia.

CAPTAIN JAMES COOK

In a third voyage, he searched the Pacific north and south and died at last on the Hawaiian Islands in 1779.

Let's think about the earth's globe now.

Around the equator is the Torrid Zone, which stretches from 23.5° N to 23.5° S. Over all this area, north and south of the equator, the sun is overhead at noon at some period during the year.

The North Temperate Zone stretches from 23.5° N to 66.5° N. In the North Temperate Zone the noonday sun is always south of overhead. It comes closer to overhead in the spring and is highest on June 21. Then it moves farther south and is lowest on December 21. The day is therefore longest and the night shortest on June 21. The day is shortest and the night longest on December 21.

The farther north one goes, the longer the days get in June and the shorter the nights. What's more, the days get shorter in December, and the nights get longer.

In the South Temperate Zone, stretching from 23.5° S to 66.5° S, everything is the opposite. The noonday sun is always north of overhead. It is closest to overhead on December 21; it moves farthest north and is lowest on June 21. The longest day and shortest night is on December 21, and the shortest day and longest night is on June 21. The farther south one goes, the longer the days and the shorter the nights on December 21; the shorter the days and the longer the nights on June 21.

North and south have winters at opposite times of years. In the North Temperate Zone it is coldest in January and February and warmest in July and August. In the South Temperate Zone, it is warmest in January and February and coldest in July and August.

North of 66.5° N, stretching all the way up to the North Pole is the Arctic Zone. There, on June 21, the day is so long that the sun stays above the horizon for twenty-four hours. The nearer you get to the North Pole, the longer it stays in the sky. When you are at the North Pole, the sun stays in the sky for half a year (though it is always near the horizon).

On December 21 in the Arctic Zone the sun doesn't show up at all for the whole day. The farther north you go, the longer it doesn't appear. At the North Pole the sun stays out of the sky for six months.

The line of 66.5° N forms a circle around the earth and is the boundary of the Arctic region. It is called the Arctic Circle.

South of the South Temperate Zone is a region that is on the opposite side of the world from the Arctic. It is just like the Arctic as far as the be-

**HOURS OF SUMMER DAYLIGHT
ABOVE THE ARCTIC CIRCLE**

12 NOON   2 PM   4 PM   6 PM   8 PM   10 PM MIDNI

havior of the sun is concerned. It is the Antarctic Zone ("opposite the Arctic").

The line of 66.5° S forms a circle around the earth. It is the boundary of the Antarctic Zone and is called the Antarctic Circle.

Inside the Antarctic Zone, the sun stays in the sky the whole day of December 21 and stays out of the sky the whole day of June 21 (just the opposite of the situation in the Arctic). The farther you go toward the South Pole, the longer the sun stays in the sky in June and the longer it stays out of the sky in December. At the South Pole the sun is the sky for six months and out of the sky for six months.

All the explorations from the time of the Portuguese navigators had never taken anyone beyond the South Temperate Zone.

On January 17, 1773, however, Captain Cook took his ship so far south that they crossed the

AM   4 AM   6 AM   8 AM   10 AM   NOON   2 PM

Antarctic Circle. He and the men on his ship were the first human beings who *ever* crossed the Antarctic Circle and who *ever* penetrated the Antarctic region.

Cook made two other crossings in the course of his journey, and his most southerly penetration took place on January 30, 1774. He then

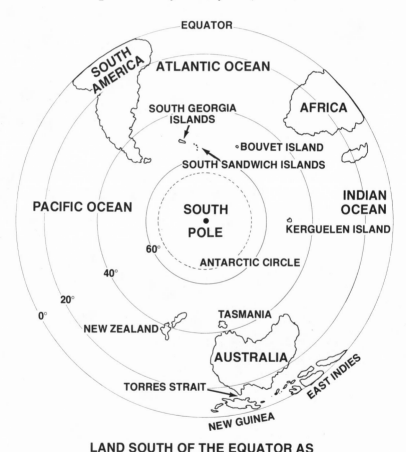

LAND SOUTH OF THE EQUATOR AS KNOWN IN 1775

reached 71.2° S. He was nearly four fifths of the way from the equator to the South Pole; he was only 1,200 miles from the South Pole.

Cook never saw land, however, when he crossed the Antarctic Circle. The farther south he went, the colder it got and the icier the ocean was. Even though Captain Cook crossed the Antarctic Circle when it was summer in the Far South, the ice stopped him before he could reach land.

In the course of his far southern voyage, Captain Cook discovered an island he called South Georgia Island (after King George III) about 1,100 miles east of Tierra del Fuego. He also discovered the South Sandwich Islands (after the earl of Sandwich, who was the head of the British Navy at this time).

South Georgia Island is about as far south as Cape Horn, but the South Sandwich Islands are farther south. They were the first pieces of land to be found that were farther south than Cape Horn. The southernmost island of the group is at 59.4° S, however, and is still in the South Temperate Zone.

Captain Cook never discovered any *land* inside the Antarctic region.

3 South to the Edge of Antarctica

As a result of Captain Cook's explorations, the far southern waters of the ocean were shown to be rich in seals and whales. Seals are valuable for their furs and whales are valuable for their fat. Ships hunting for seals and whales flocked southward. Explorers did so also.

A British naval officer, William Smith, discovered the South Shetland Islands (named for the Shetland Islands north of Scotland) in October 1819. These are directly south of South Georgia, and the most southerly island of the group is at 63° S. It was the most southerly piece of land discovered up to that time, but it was still in the South Temperate Zone.

The British naval commander, Edward Bransfield, charted the South Shetland Islands and then went farther south to 64.5° S. On

January 30, 1820, he may have seen land there. The waters between the South Shetland Islands and the land to the south are still called Bransfield Strait in his honor.

Later that year, on November 16, 1820, a twenty-one-year-old American, Nathaniel Brown Palmer, in command of a small ship that was part of a larger fleet hunting seals, definitely sighted land south of Bransfield Strait.

The land sighted by Bransfield and by Palmer was part of a long thin S-shaped peninsula. The Americans called it Palmer Land, but the British, who insisted Bransfield saw it first, called it Graham Land in honor of James Graham, who was head of the British Navy at that time.

It wasn't till 1964 that the argument was settled. The land is now called Antarctic Peninsula.

Bransfield and Palmer were the first human beings in history ever to sight any part of a large body of land, but they didn't know what they had done.

On February 7, 1821, an American seal hunter, John Davis, actually set foot on the Antarctic Peninsula. This fact was not known till the log of his ship was discovered and studied in 1955. Davis expressed the opinion in the log that the land was part of an Antarctic continent, but he had no real evidence for that. Still, he was the first human being who ever stood on it.

The part of the Antarctic Peninsula that Bransfield, Palmer, and Davis were involved with is not in the Antarctic region, however. The peninsula juts northward a considerable distance into the South Temperate Zone. In fact, the northernmost part of the Antarctic Peninsula is at 63° S, about 250 miles north of the Antarctic Circle.

The Russians were busy exploring the Arctic regions in the Far North, and they thought it might be interesting to look into the Antarctic, too.

In 1819 the Russian tsar, Alexander I, sent a navigator, Fabian Gottlieb Bellingshausen (BEL-ings-HOW-zen), southward. Bellingshausen had orders to go farther south than the mark Captain Cook had reached.

Bellingshausen did his best, but the ice stopped him short of Captain Cook's mark. Bellingshausen came across a small island, however, which he named Peter I Island after the Russian tsar Peter the Great.

Peter I Island is at 68.8° S, or 150 miles *south* of the Antarctic Circle. It was the very first piece of land ever found inside the Antarctic region.

Bellingshausen then discovered a larger island just west of the Antarctic Peninsula and named it for the tsar who sent him. It is Alexander I Island, and it turned out to be the largest island in the Antarctic region, or, in fact, anywhere south of Cape Horn.

It is not certain if Bellingshausen actually saw the Antarctic continent or not. It is hard to tell if a distant shelf of ice is just ice or if it has land under it. If he *did* see the continent, he may have

FABIAN VON BELLINGSHAUSEN

been the first one to do so.

Perhaps it is best to divide the credit and not argue about it. We can say that Palmer of the United States, Bransfield of Great Britain, and Bellingshausen of Russia all saw pieces of it before the end of 1820.

The important thing to remember, though, is that none of the three had any way of telling whether any land they saw was really part of a continent or was just an island. Davis said it was part of a continent, but he was just guessing. He had no evidence.

In 1823 Captain Cook's southern mark was finally broken. An English whaling ship, under James Weddell, found a stretch of ocean that extended farther south than anything explored before. On February 20, 1823, Weddell reached a mark of 72.25° S before winds and ice turned him back.

This was a new record. Weddell had approached to within 1,120 miles of the South Pole.

The portion of the ocean into which Weddell had sailed lies east of the Antarctic Peninsula and is known as Weddell Sea in his honor.

Weddell suspected that the sea in this region penetrated all the way to the South Pole and that it was only the ice that would prevent a ship from sailing there. Actually, this proved not to be so in later years. The southernmost reach of Weddell Sea is at 76° S, and at that point there is a shoreline that is still 840 miles from the South Pole.

All the discoveries of the 1820s in the neighborhood of the Antarctic Circle were made in the general area south of Tierra del Fuego. In 1831 the first sighting of Antarctic land on the other side of the Antarctic region was made.

In that year, an English navigator, John Briscoe, saw a shoreline far to the south of Africa. It was about 60 miles north of the Antarctic Circle, so it was still in the South Temperate Zone. He called it Enderby Land after the owners of his vessel. He saw it from a distance, though. Ice prevented him from actually reaching it.

In 1840, the French explorer, Jules Dumont d'Urville (dyoor-VEEL), sailed south from Australia and spied a shoreline almost exactly on the Antarctic Circle. He named it Adélie Land (uh-DAY-lee) after his wife.

At almost the same time, an American explorer, Charles Wilkes, was steering his ship along a long stretch of coastline between Enderby Land and Adélie Land, a coastline that followed the curve of the Antarctic Circle almost exactly. This stretch of coast, lying south of the Indian Ocean, is now known as Wilkes Land.

Wilkes, on returning, was the first to show that all the different discoveries of the previous twenty years could be fitted together to show the existence of an Antarctic continent.

His arguments were very convincing, and explorers accepted them. The southern continent was all in the Antarctic region, however, so that it had to be covered by ice. It was not a continent that human beings could live on. To this day, the only human beings who are to be found on it are explorers and scientists who are only there temporarily.

A natural name for the continent was Antarctica.

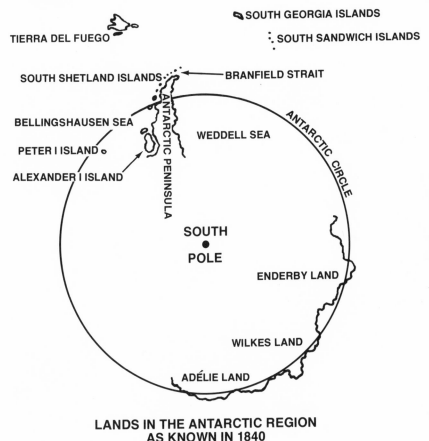

**LANDS IN THE ANTARCTIC REGION
AS KNOWN IN 1840**

4 South to the South Pole

ONCE ANTARCTICA WAS DISCOVERED, exploration went on more extensively than ever. People wanted to find out all the details of the new continent.

In January 1841 a Scottish explorer, James Clark Ross, entered an ocean inlet along the Antarctic coast. This inlet lay to the south of New Zealand, and it is called Ross Sea in his honor.

Its western shore Ross named Victoria Land after the British Queen who had just begun her reign four years before. Along that western shore was a mountain range, which he called Prince Albert Mountains after Victoria's husband.

Ross sailed south into Ross Sea till he found himself stopped by a towering wall of ice two hundred to three hundred feet high. This turned out to be an ice shelf. It had been formed on land

41

JAMES CLARK ROSS

and had been forced outward onto the sea as more ice continually formed on top of it.

The thick ice shelf filled most of Ross Sea. This Ross Ice Shelf, as it is now called, covers an area equal to that of the nation of France.

At the point where Ross encountered the ice shelf, there is a piece of land now known as Ross Island. On it, Ross discovered, on January 27, 1841, two volcanoes, which he named Mount Erebus and Mount Terror after his two ships. Mount Erebus is the taller of the two and is 2.3 miles high. It is an active volcano, the most southerly active volcano in the world.

To the east of Ross Island, the open sea extended somewhat farther south than to the west. This inlet Ross called McMurdo Bay after the first mate of one of his ships.

Ross explored along the Ross Ice Shelf for about 450 miles before leaving Antarctica. In 1842 he visited Ross Sea again and reached a new southern record of 78.15° S. This is only 700 miles from the South Pole.

If we could imagine the Ross Ice Shelf disappearing, it would be seen that the Ross Sea extends farther south than any other part of the world's oceans. At its farthest south it is at 86° S, about 300 miles from the South Pole.

By the middle of the 1800s it was clear that the South Pole was located on the continent of Antarctica and the Ross's southern mark was as far south as it was possible to go by ship. Anyone

MOUNT EREBUS

who wanted to get closer to the South Pole than that would have to go overland.

But there wasn't really any land on Antarctica, only ice. It isn't easy to travel long distances over ice. For years after Ross's voyage, ships kept nosing around Antarctica without anyone ever setting foot on the continent.

Finally, at the beginning of 1895, a Norwegian whaling ship, commanded by Leonard Kristenson (KRIS-ten-sun), visited Victoria Land on the rim of the Ross Sea. There, on January 23, 1895, a party alighted and stood on Antarctica.

Of course, Davis had stood upon Antarctica seventy years before, but no one knew that in 1895. Besides, Davis had stood on Antarctic Peninsula, which curves north into the South Temperate Zone. Kristenson and his party were the first human beings *ever* to stand on Antarctica inside the Antarctic Circle.

One of the party was a Norwegian named Carsten E. Borchgrevink (BORK-gray-vink). He returned in 1898 and, with nine other men, spent the whole winter along the Antarctic coast. This was the first time that anyone had ever visited the continent during its winter season.

In the Antarctic summer of 1900 Borchgrevink returned, and this time he decided to do more than just stand on Antarctica. He left his ship, put on skis, and sped southward. It was the first time anyone had actually tried to travel on Antarctica.

On February 16, 1900, Borchgrevink reached a point that was at 78.8° S, only 685 miles from the South Pole. He had finally broken Ross's record after sixty years.

After that, every expedition to Antarctica put men onshore on the Ross Ice Shelf. Person after person tried to break the record and go farther south than anyone else had ever gone. The ambition was to be the first person to reach the South Pole.

One person who was particularly anxious to set the record was a British explorer, Robert Falcon Scott.

Naturally, you can't just walk southward over the ice, or even ski southward for long distances. You have to have food, fuel, tents, and other supplies with you, or you will simply starve or freeze to death before you have gone very far.

That means you have to take along sledges— vehicles on runners. On the sledges are your supplies. Either you must pull the sledges as you go, or you must have animals to pull them. Dogs with thick coats of hair, used to cold weather, are best.

Toward the end of 1902 Scott entered Ross Sea and named the land along its eastern shore Edward VII Land after the just crowned king of England. Scott and his colleagues then pulled sledges over the Ross Ice Shelf. On December 13, 1902, they reached 82.28° S, only 500 miles from the South Pole.

In January 1909 one of Scott's colleagues, a British explorer named Ernest Shackleton, made another try for the South Pole. On January 9, 1909, his party of four men, each man dragging a sledge, managed to reach 88.38° S, only 100 miles from the South Pole.

There, they were forced to turn back. If they had traveled farther, their food supply would not have lasted the return journey. They did manage to show, though, that the South Pole was located on a high plateau.

All was set now for the final push. Scott was going to make one more try. A Norwegian explorer named Roald Amundsen (AH-moonsen), who had done a lot of exploring in the regions of the Arctic, was also set to try.

Amundsen prepared very carefully and used more dogs than anyone else ever had in the Antarctic region. He had fifty-two dogs to pull the sledges which carried everything he needed. He began to cross the Ross Ice Shelf on October 20,

ROALD AMUNDSEN

1911. As he proceeded, he killed the weaker dogs and fed them to the others. In this way the food supplies he brought were saved for the human members of the expedition and there was no danger of running out of food.

Amundsen reached the South Pole on December 14, 1911. He left a marker there, and he and his men were back at their ship on January 21, 1912, with twelve dogs still surviving and with plenty of food still left. All the members of the expedition had returned safely and in good health.

Scott's attempt was less carefully organized

and he did not supply himself with as many dogs. By the last 400 miles Scott's party had to pull their own sledges.

They finally reached the South Pole on January 17, 1912, but they found Amundsen's marker there. They had lost the race. It had taken them sixty-nine days to reach the South Pole, and it had only taken Amundsen fifty-five days.

Scott and his four companions were worn out, but they couldn't stop to rest. They had to get back as quickly as possible, or they would run out of food. On the way back, however, all five were caught in a blizzard that went on and on for nine days. All died of cold on or about March 29, 1912.

Meanwhile, a German explorer, Wilhelm Filchner (FILK-ner), explored Weddell Sea and found in its southern reaches an ice shelf as large as the Ross Ice Shelf. This second one is the Filchner Ice Shelf.

If the ice shelves are ignored, Ross Sea and Weddell Sea would approach each other with just a 600-mile stretch of land lying between. This would be an isthmus connecting two parts of Antarctica.

The two parts, East Antarctica and West Antarctica, are unequal in size. West Antarctica, which lies south of the American continents, possesses an irregular coastline and includes the Antarctic Peninsula. It makes up only about one third of the continent.

East Antarctica has a nearly semicircular shoreline running almost exactly along the Antarctic Circle. It lies south of Africa, Asia, and Australia.

Crossing the isthmus and running along the eastern shores of Ross Sea and Weddell Sea is Antarctica's greatest mountain range, the Transantarctic Mountains. One of its peaks is Mount Fridtjof Nansen (frit-yuf-NAN-sen), named for a Norwegian who had explored the Arctic region. It is 3.6 miles high, the tallest peak in Antarctica.

ADMIRAL RICHARD E. BYRD

**ADMIRAL RICHARD E. BYRD'S PLANE
LANDING ON LITTLE AMERICA**

In the years immediately after the South Pole
had been reached, an Australian explorer, Doug-
las Mawson, carefully mapped just about the en-
tire Antarctic coast.

The first air flight over Antarctica was made on
December 20, 1928.

This was something new in exploration. An
airplane could cover great distances in very short
periods of time. It was no longer necessary to
make a dangerous and difficult journey on foot if
you didn't want to.

In 1929 the American explorer, Richard Evelyn Byrd, flew from the Antarctica shore to the South Pole and back in one day, covering a round-trip distance of 1,600 miles. He established a base he named Little America on the eastern edge of the Ross Ice Shelf, near Roosevelt Island.

In 1934 Byrd wintered alone in a tiny base 125 miles south of Little America. It was the first time any man had spent the winter in the antarctic interior.

In 1935 an Australian explorer, Hubert Wil-

kins, and an American, Lincoln Ellsworth, flew all the way across from one shore of the continent to the opposite shore, making a trip that was 2,300 miles long.

In 1939 an expedition headed by Byrd mapped 135,000 square miles of Antarctica by means of plane flights.

Finally, in 1957, a party under the leadership of Vivian Fuchs (FYOOKS) made a successful crossing of the continent from shore to shore, on land.

The exploration of Antarctica, geographically at least, was just about complete. Only details remain to be filled in.

5 Life on Antarctica

WHEN ANTARCTICA WAS STUDIED from the air, no one was surprised to find it was all covered by ice. The layer of ice that covers it is one and a half times as large as the United States and is well over a mile thick on the average. In some places it is two and a half miles thick.

There is nine times as much ice in Antarctica as in all the rest of the earth combined.

There are bare patches here and there along the Antarctic shore, however. The largest bare patch is at the eastern edge of the Ross Ice Shelf. There is a bit of exposed ground there that is about 90 miles long and 12 miles wide.

There are a few bare patches in the interior of Antarctica, too. Some of the mountaintops are blown free of snow and stand bare under the sky.

There are even some ice-free spots here and there in the valleys. Scientists aren't sure why they are ice-free. All the bare spots in Antarctica have an area of about 3,000 square miles altogether. This is a little over half the size of the state of Connecticut.

The southernmost of these bare spots is on

RESEARCH STATION ON ANTARCTIC PENINSULA

Mount Howe, and it is only 160 miles from the South Pole.

Perhaps the bare spots are kept free of ice because of heat from underground. In some of the valleys there are small ponds of water that stay liquid all through the terrible Antarctic winter. In 1947 one airplane spotted a bare spot in which there were twenty-three separate ponds of water.

The ponds aren't large. One, San Juan Pond, isn't much larger than a football stadium and the water is only six inches deep. All the water in San Juan Pond would fill six average-size American living rooms.

There is almost no life in the interior of Antarctica. There is none on the ice. In the lakes and on the bare ground there are some very simple plants, such as algae, lichens, and moss. There are two hundred kinds of algae found in Antarctica, four hundred kinds of lichens, and seventy-five kinds of moss. San Juan Pond contains nothing but one kind of bacterium.

There are even two kinds of flowering plants found on Antarctic Peninsula, which juts into the South Temperate Zone.

Lichens have been detected on bare rock as close as 260 miles from the South Pole. That is the closest that life on the ground has come to the South Pole, except for human beings and whatever other life forms human beings have brought with them.

There is even less animal life on Antarctica than there is plant life. The only land animals native to Antarctica are seventy kinds of insects and mites. (Mites are small members of the spider family.) The largest Antarctic animal is a wingless fly about an eighth of an inch long. Mites have been detected only 425 miles from the South Pole.

Though there is almost no life in Antarctica itself, the ocean off its shores is rich in life. There are myriad tiny plants in the upper layers of the cold ocean, and animals of all kinds from microscopic cells to giant whales.

The blue whale lives in the ocean off Antarctica. It is the largest animal that has ever lived on planet Earth. It can be one hundred feet long and weigh 150 tons.

Some animals that live on fish spend time on the shores of Antarctica and have their young there. These include five kinds of seals. The most southerly of these is the Weddell seal,

WEDDELL SEAL

which sticks very close to shore at all times. It can usually be found beneath the ice in the coastal waters. It breaks holes in the ice through which it breathes.

There are fifteen kinds of flying birds that live on the fish off the Antarctic coast. The most southerly of these is a kind of gull called the *skua*. It flies long distances over Antarctica and probably has flown over the South Pole. If so, it is the only living thing to have reached the South Pole without the help of human beings.

There are two kinds of flightless birds called penguins that live in Antarctica. Though they can't use their wings for flying, those wings make wonderful paddles for swimming. Penguins can swim 30 miles an hour under water, and they can twist and turn with great skill.

One of the Antarctic penguins is the *Adélie*

SKUA

ADÉLIE PENGUINS

penguin, which is called that because it is found in Adélie Land. The Adélie penguin stands about twenty inches tall and weighs about fifteen pounds. These penguins make their homes along patches of bare ground near the shore.

The other Antarctic penguin is the largest of all living penguins. It is the *emperor penguin,* which can be nearly four feet high and can weigh as much as seventy-five pounds.

Emperor penguins have the strangest nesting habits of any bird in the world. They collect into crowded "rookeries" in order to lay their eggs. There are now known to be fourteen rookeries with an average of about eleven thousand birds in each.

The rookeries are located about 50 to 80 miles

EMPEROR PENGUINS

inland. The emperor penguins get their food along the shore, of course, since they live on fish. When it comes time to lay eggs, they must walk to the rookeries. It takes them a month to walk there.

Once they start their walk, there is no more food available, so they go the month without eating.

It is the beginning of winter when they reach the rookery and there the female lays a single egg. There is no nest. The single egg is taken by the male, who places it on his feet immediately under a bare and unfeathered patch on his abdomen. A flap of skin covers the egg and keeps it warm.

Once the egg is laid, the female leaves and travels back to the sea, which means another month's journey without food.

The male penguin stays in the rookery for two months of the Antarctic winter, keeping the egg warm. Before he came to the rookery, the male penguin had put on as much fat as possible, and now he must live on this fat.

Thousands of the male penguins huddle together, each with his egg, while the Antarctic temperatures go as low as −60° C (−75° F) and frigid gales whistle past at speeds up to 90 miles an hour. Those penguins on the outside of the swarm, who are exposed to the wind and cold, keep pushing their way into it in order to keep warmer. Others are forced onto the outside and begin to push inward in their turn. Every penguin gets his turn at being outside and inside.

When the eggs are near to hatching, the females return and take over. At last the males can head for the sea, which they finally reach after their four-month fast. During that fast they lose 25 to 40 percent of their weight.

When the egg hatches, the mother penguin must feed the chick with food it has stored in its crop, but this won't last. The father must return. The parents take turns walking to the sea, eating as much as they can and returning to feed the chick.

Finally, by the time the Antarctic winter is over, the baby penguins that have survived are big enough to march to the sea and begin to feed themselves.

It's a hard life, but the emperor penguin has complete security inland. While it is hatching and raising its chick, there is no animal that can threaten to eat them. Only people can come near them.

And people are constantly on Antarctica now, studying it. There are traces of ancient animals there that existed when Antarctica was located in milder parts of the world before it moved to the South Pole many millions of years ago. There are coal beds there, too.

What's more, the huge chunks of ice that break off into the ocean around the rim of Antarctica may be important sources of fresh water some day. Antarctica may not be much of a vacation spot, but the time may come when it will be very useful to humanity.